Foreword

When Fordham University researchers Bruce Cooper, Lance Fusarelli, and Vin Carella called AASA about doing a survey of the job expectations and future needs of superintendents in the United States, we were happy to assist them. We too are concerned about a free, open, and robust flow of high-quality candidates into the top leadership role in American education.

The survey asked superintendents to share their feelings about education leadership, their career goals and accomplishments, and their perceptions of the supply of superintendent candidates. We wanted to look at other constraints on a vigorous, open market for superintendents, including loss of a relative pay advantage, inability to transport a vested pension plan across state lines, insecurity in the job, segmentation of the market, lack of interest in applying for jobs in large urban and inner-city districts, and the skills superintendents bring to the office.

For all the pressures and constraints associated with school district leadership, this survey indicates that superintendents possess a firm, long-term commitment to leadership in education, with respondents holding their current job an average of 7.4 years. The demography of the superintendency remains essentially static: the typical leader is a white male in his 50s. Most have doctorates, although this is less true in rural and smaller districts where school leaders may have less access to advanced degree programs and perhaps less demand for that degree from hiring boards.

We appear to be at the edge of a sea change. When these middle-aged, white male superintendents call it quits, and a large number are retirement-eligible, we can expect to see more women, minorities, and younger leaders taking their places. Already, the percent of female superintendents has risen from 7 in 1992 to 12 in 1999, and it's currently nearly 20 percent in the largest 88 districts surveyed.

The picture that emerges in this study is one of a potential future crisis. Superintendents of this generation are doing their job, but they worry, as we all do, about the next cohort of leaders.

Can the position of superintendent be a satisfying career? Yes, most agree, it can.

Would sitting superintendents recommend the position to a younger colleague interested in educational leadership? Yes, but with some reservations.

Can the position be strengthened through restructuring; more support; better pay, benefits, and pension opportunities; and more rewards and recognition? Yes, again.

Can the next generation of top leaders be adequately recruited, prepared, inducted, and maintained? That is the challenge that faces us, as we continue to think about and advocate quality leadership for our schools.

Paul D. Houston, Executive Director
American Association of School Administrators

List of Tables

EXECUTIVE SUMMARY

CAREER CRISIS IN THE SCHOOL SUPERINTENDENCY?

The Results of a National Survey

Bruce S. Cooper   Lance D. Fusarelli   Vincent A. Carella

INTRODUCTION

Is the school superintendency still an attractive, workable profession for educators dedicated to school reform? The popular perception of the superintendency is that of an impossible job few want to undertake in which even the best and the brightest confront escalating and competing demands, find themselves besieged by confusing and conflicting interest groups, and enjoy little or no job security. But for all the speculation and concern about the position, *superintendents themselves are rarely asked what they think about the position, career crises, job mobility, role satisfaction, and future life plans.*

This study, conducted with support from the American Association of School Administrators (AASA) and technical advice on questionnaire design from the National Center for Education Statistics (NCES), explores the views of public school superintendents. A new, validated survey instrument, *SPEAR™ (Superintendents' Professional Expectations and Advancement Review)*, asked these top executives about their opinions, skills, perceptions of a range of career concerns, and future interests.

Of the nation's some 13,500 school superintendents, we selected a random sample of 2,979 segmented by district size: 171 of the largest school systems (those with over 25,000 pupils); 1,754 districts with between 24,999 and 2,500 students, and 1,054 districts with fewer than 2,499 students. We had a return rate of 57.7 percent; of the 1,719 questionnaires returned, 88 were from respondents in the largest districts, 1,042 from the medium size districts, and 589 from the smallest districts.

Some of our findings were surprising to us. Our overall finding is that superintendents are proud and satisfied with their own accomplishments, but greatly concerned about the prospect of finding talented leaders to take their places.

FINDINGS

Our survey explored the following questions, which are presented here with a brief description of our findings.

I. **Is there a crisis in attracting educators into the profession?** *Yes indeed.* 88 percent of superintendents polled agreed that the "shortage of applicants for the superintendent's job is a serious crisis in American education." Furthermore, 92 percent are concerned that "high turnover in the superintendency means a serious crisis in keeping strong leaders in the position"; this despite the fact that respondents have an average of 30 years service in education, with more than 7 years tenure in their current post -- a sign of job continuity and stability. It is interesting that even respondents whose own careers seem to involve long service, hard work, and a willingness to recommend the position to others are concerned about their profession and its future.

II. **How satisfied are superintendents with their careers, and would they recommend the job to younger, up-and-coming educators?** Respondents indicate great concern about the position, not so much in this generation but for the next. As the cohort of current leaders ages, those surveyed worry about where the next generation will come from. However, the current superintendents find the work challenging, rewarding, and satisfying, particularly in building curriculum, helping students, and contributing to society.

III. **How mobile are school superintendents?** *Not very.* The group of superintendents now in office have served their time: 30 years on average in education; 15 or so in the superintendency. They don't see themselves as mobile, but are willing to pass the baton to the next generation. Why is the current group not very mobile itself? Several factors restrict their mobility:

• **Considering a job in another district:** Only 18 percent expressed interest in a superintendency in large, urban school districts, stating that they were "definitely" or "somewhat" interested; 93 percent of respondents are attracted to districts "similar to where they now work."

• **Segmentation of the job market:** Only 51 percent are willing to consider "a good job" in another district, if one were available. Thus, the market appears only moderately attractive and strongly segmented, limiting mobility across types of districts.

• **Inequitable professional training:** Only 43 percent of respondents in small, primarily rural districts have attained their doctorate, compared to 79 percent in large districts and 75 percent in medium-sized systems. Thus, rural superintendents without doctoral degrees may be passed over for positions in larger suburban and urban districts; or those without the doctorate may select rural jobs – indicating that the causality may go both ways.

• **Non-portability of pensions:** 86 percent of superintendents are vested in their current jobs, while only 18 percent are vested in more than one state. Because their pension plans are not portable from one state to another, superintendents (79 percent of whom are over 50 years old) are constrained in job searches to the state where they currently work.

IV. What are the professional concerns of superintendents? *Varies.*

• **Emotional Support:** 90 percent of superintendents agree that districts should give them "more help and support to ensure their well-being and job success."

• **Better Pay and Benefits:** Similarly, 90 percent assert that higher pay and benefits are "a strong incentive to candidates in considering a career in the superintendency."

• **More Professional Development:** Eighty-one percent want more money to attend professional meetings; 74 percent want more training and counseling from universities and other institutions. Only about half of superintendents, 49 percent, believe that tenure would make the superintendency more attractive.

V. What personal concerns and motives are expressed by superintendents? *Varies.*

• **Job Satisfaction:** A vast majority, 91 percent, agree strongly that "my work in this district has given me real career satisfaction." However, in looking toward the future, only 65 percent indicate that they would "truly recommend the profession of superintendent as a meaningful and satisfying career" to a fellow educator. Thus, while superintendents themselves feel satisfied, they are hesitant to entice others into the field.

• **To Make a Difference in the Lives of Students:** A vast majority, 96 percent, agree that their work made "a significant difference in the lives of children."

VI. What skills do superintendents bring to the job? *People skills; general skills.*

• **Human and Community Relations:** Almost all, 99 percent of respondents self-reported "High/Moderate" human relations skills; 93 percent believe themselves skilled in community relations. In contrast, only 86 percent believe they have "High to Moderate" skills in the area of technology, and 65 percent in race relations.

• **General Expertise:** A majority of respondents self-reported "High/Moderate" expertise in the areas of building construction/bond issues (89 percent), labor relations (87 percent), curriculum design (82 percent), and finance/budgeting (97 percent).

RECOMMENDATIONS

Based on the findings in this report, the following recommendations seem necessary to improve the attractiveness of the superintendency, and thus increase the pool of candidates for this important position.

• **De-segment the Job Market**: Encourage easier access across the job market by types of districts; open up the market.

• **Reorganize the Superintendency**: Superintendents want more support and clearer expectations, and better pay. Respondents want to move away from a strictly management role to a more supportive one.

• **Make Pensions More Portable**: Initiatives should guarantee regional or national reciprocity for pension plans, much like the university model whereby university faculty can work at any U.S. university and the vesting and pension "follows" the employee.

• **Expand and Improve Doctoral Programs**: Sixty-four percent of superintendents overall in the United States have their doctorate, but only 43 percent of leaders in rural and smaller districts have the Ed.D. or Ph.D. To improve and equalize access to advanced graduate degrees, states and communities, in collaboration with universities, should extend opportunities to school leaders in all types of communities to engage in graduate work through paid leave, distance learning, and special programs.

• **Improve Economic Benefits**: Superintendents are suffering from a lack of salary increases relative to raises for teachers and principals. Adjustments should be made to make the top jobs more attractive.

• **Increase Opportunities for Women and Minorities**: The lack of female (only 12 percent in this survey) and minority superintendents (only 6 percent in the survey) remains a continuing professional concern. More active efforts to recruit women and minorities into the superintendency should be undertaken.

• **Enhance Superintendents' Technical Skills**: Preparation programs should help superintendents improve their knowledge of technology and systems analysis.

• **Value, Recognize, and Reward Superintendents' Contributions**: State, regional, and national organizations should do more to recognize outstanding superintendents. In addition to overall "superintendent of the year" awards, associations should highlight "best practices" in vital areas such as improved standards, new technology, alignment of assessment, curriculum, and instructional leadership. Visible, meaningful rewards are powerful incentives to motivate incumbents to improve and to draw new talent into the superintendency well into the 21st century.

For more information, please contact the authors:

Bruce S. Cooper
Fordham University School of Education
26 East 10th Street 9C
New York, NY 10003
TEL: 212-254-1192, FAX: 212-673-5426
e-mail: bscooperph@AOL.com

Lance D. Fusarelli
Fordham University School of Education
113 West 60th St., Suite 1119
New York, NY 10023
TEL: 212-636-6438, FAX: 212-636-7875

Vincent A. Carella
Somers High School
120 Primrose St., Rt. 139
Lincolndale, NY 10540
Office Tel: 914-248-8585
Home Address: 100 Church St., Nanuet, NY 10454
Home Tel: 914-623-1987

Career Crisis in the School Superintendency?

The Results of a National Survey

Bruce S. Cooper   Lance D. Fusarelli   Vincent A. Carella
Fordham University   Fordham University   Lincolndale, NY, Public Schools

*   *   *

School superintendents around the country have been quitting in droves and have been dismissed or have retired early, often because they failed to deliver the quick fixes demanded of them. ... And the searches for superintendents are getting harder. Cities are finding fewer and fewer candidates willing to apply for these jobs, despite salaries that in many cases top $100,000 per year.

(S. Daly, *New York Times. 12/26/90*)

The superintendency requires "fire in the belly," physical stamina, leadership skills, vision, and a strong desire to use one's power to improve the lives of children.   (Carter and Cunningham, 1997, p. 4)

*   *   *

Introduction

Is the school superintendent becoming an endangered species? Is the superintendency in crisis if not meltdown? Paul D. Houston, executive director of the American Association of School Administrators (AASA), laments that "administrators who may be considering the superintendency look at those already in those roles, see how unbalanced their lives often are, and say, 'Thanks but no thanks!'" (Houston, 1998, p. 44). Anecdotal evidence suggests that when top education jobs are advertised, fewer candidates apply than a few years ago. Ironically, this is occurring just as the nation recognizes the full value of education and the need for school reform.

The popular perception of the superintendency is that of an impossible job few want to undertake in which even the best and the brightest confront escalating and competing demands, find themselves besieged by confusing and conflicting interest groups, and enjoy little or no job security. One senses that superintendents are certainly "targets of criticisms, centers of controversy, defenders of policies, and orchestrators of diverse interests" (Norton et al., 1996, p. 21). Or, as Robert Crowson (1987) so aptly explains, "the superintendency is a position strangely awash in contradictions and anomalies, and frankly, a distinct puzzle to those who seek to make a bit of conceptual sense out of this intriguing job" (pp. 49-50). Kowalski (1995) writes that "it is ironic that coaches in professional sports often are accorded more opportunity to succeed than big city superintendents" (p. 152).

Yet, for all the talk, concerns, and myths about career expectations and advancement of the nation's top education leaders, little hard information is available on how *superintendents themselves* view their job mobility, role satisfaction, and future life plans. With invaluable help from the American Association of School Administrators (AASA) and technical advice from the survey unit at the National Center for Education Statistics (NCES), we designed and validated a new instrument, the *Superintendents' Professional Expectations & Advancement Review (SPEAR*™*)* (See Appendix A). Our goal was to survey incumbent superintendents from around the nation to find out what these chief executives think about their careers and what is happening to their role as school district leaders.

The survey was mailed by AASA to 2,979 randomly selected superintendents, AASA members as well as non-members, stratified to include a higher percentage of the school districts with the most students because these men and women represent the majority of students in the United States. We expected, optimistically, a 10 percent return rate, given the excessive amount of mail coming across the superintendent's desk, the length and depth of the questionnaire (5 pages, nearly 70 items), and the tendency of people to chuck unannounced surveys into the trash can.

Amazingly, 1,719 superintendents (57.7 percent of those who were mailed the survey) from school districts of all sizes, locations, and types, responded to *SPEAR*^TM, perhaps indicating superintendents' need and desire to communicate about their careers.

District Size	Sample Size	Number & Percent Returned	
25,000 pupils or more	171 districts	88 districts	51.5%
24,999-2,500 pupils	1,754 districts	1,042 districts	59.4%
2,499 or fewer pupils	1,054 districts	589 districts	55.9%
All districts:	2,979 districts	1,719 districts	57.7%

The survey was a complex inquiry into the nature of the nation's school superintendency. It explored leaders' backgrounds and experiences, their perceptions of the role in general, their areas of expertise, the constraints on their careers (economic, familial, personal, and organizational), their mobility, and the kinds of districts in which they would most and least like to work.

Career in Crisis?

An important question explored in the study is whether the nation's superintendents believe their position is in crisis. Respondents were asked about their sense of "crisis" in the superintendency nationally – not just in their own particular district or type of district.

SPEAR^{TM} Items: Respondents were asked to rate three statements related to the career crisis on a 5-point Likert scale in which 5 = Strongly Agree and 1 = Strongly Disagree.

The first statement was "The shortage of applicants for the superintendents' job is a serious crisis in American education." The next item probed the "quality of candidates" for these positions; "A crisis in school leadership is created by the low quality of candidates for the superintendency." And the third item was "High turnover for the superintendency means a serious crisis in keeping strong leaders in the position."

As shown in Table 1, the average score for all superintendents (N=1,717) on the shortage crisis item was 4.35 out of a possible 5.0, meaning that most respondents "agreed strongly" or "agreed somewhat" that the nation is facing a shortage of applicants for top executive slots. When we compare by district size, the crisis appears slightly more serious to respondents in the larger districts than superintendents in the smaller districts. In other words, although all superintendents perceive a candidate shortage, those in the largest districts believe the shortage is most severe.

Table 1
Superintendents' Perceptions of Job Crisis *

	All Superintendents (N=1,717) Mean	Large Districts (n=88) Mean	Medium Districts (n=1,041) Mean	Small Districts (n=588) Mean
1. Shortage Crisis	4.35	4.45	4.36	4.31
2. Low Quality Crisis	3.39	3.45	3.44	3.30
3. Turnover Crisis	4.53	4.65	4.55	4.48
1. & 3. Overall Quality Crisis	4.48	4.55	4.46	4.39
1. - 3. Total Crisis	4.10	4.19	4.12	4.03

*Sample size (N=) varies according to number of responses per item; missing values were factored into the analysis.

The second item, "A crisis in school leadership is created by the low quality of candidates for the superintendency," did not receive the Agree Strongly that the other "crisis" items did. At 3.39, the average response was a whole point lower than to the other items. The response on the "quality" issue showed the highest level of agreement *across* districts that the low quality of applicants is a problem.

Superintendents indicated the greatest concern for the effects of high turnove*r* on strong leadership, with a mean of 4.53 overall. Again, the amount of concern seems directly related to district size.

The bottom row of Table 1 is the overall average for the three measures of crisis: shortage, quality, and turnover. Because many superintendents did not "agree strongly=5" or "agree somewhat=4" that the problem was "the low quality of candidates for the superintendency," the "quality of candidates" item reduced the total "crisis" sub-scale measure to overall 4.10. The sub-scale mean for largest systems was, again, at 4.19, medium next at 4.12, and small was lowest on the composite crisis measure at 4.03. As district size increases, superintendents' perceived sense of job crisis also increases.

Looking at the data, it is clear that respondents, who average about 7 years in their own current positions, *perceive* a crisis in terms of a shortage of candidates, turnover of strong leadership, and, to a lesser extent, poor candidate quality. These perceptual data may explain why fewer educators are seeking top positions when available, and underscores that keeping leaders in their jobs is a real problem, particularly in large urban districts.

Yet another way of displaying these same data is to use frequencies and percentages, rather than averages and standard deviations. Table 2 shows that 1,501 or 87.8 percent of the 1,709 school superintendents in this national survey "agree strongly" (50.0%) or "agree somewhat (37.8%) that the applicant shortage poses a crisis. Among the largest district leaders, *not a single respondent* disagreed with the problem statement, while only 2.9 percent of the smallest district leaders indicated "disagreement" with the shortage crisis statement in the *SPEAR*^TM instrument. Superintendents from medium-sized districts had the highest agreement about the crisis of candidates, at 89.0 percent (924 out of 1,038 respondents), while only 2.2 percent or 23 superintendents indicated that they disagree with the statement.

Table 2—Superintendents' Beliefs About Crisis in Superintendency by District Size

	All Superintendents (N=1,709) Frequency %	Large Districts (n=87) Frequency %	Medium Districts (n=1,038) Frequency %	Small Districts (n=584) Frequency %
Agree Strongly	854 (50.0%)	48 (55.2%)	518 (49.9%)	288 (49.3%)
Agree Somewhat	647 (37.8%)	30 (34.5%)	406 (39.1%)	211 (36.1%)
TOTAL AGREE	**1,501 (87.8%)**	**78 (89.7%)**	**924 (89.0%)**	**499 (85.4%)**
Neither Agree nor Disagree	168 (9.8%)	9 (10.3%)	91 (8.8%)	68 (11.6)
Disagree Somewhat	31 (1.8%)	0	20 (1.9%)	11 (1.9%)
Disagree Strongly	9 (0.5%)	0	3 (.3%)	6 (1.0%)
TOTAL DISAGREE	**40 (2.3%)**	**0**	**23 (2.2%)**	**17 (2.9%)**
Total	1,709 (100.0%)	87 (100.0%)	1,038 (100.0%)	584 (100.0%)

Whichever way we present the information, the nation's superintendents clearly agree that we face a crisis in attracting candidates for their jobs, thus increasing the need to reform the job to make it more attractive and secure. Job improvements should increase the flow of new, talented candidates into the position. School districts need to throw out a wider net to appeal to nontraditional candidates such as women, minorities, and even candidates from outside the education field. As Bok (1992) explains, "The pipeline will run almost empty and those in it will remain ill-prepared for the job" (p. 48), given the job complexity and mounting demands on the superintendent.

Superintendent Mobility? _____

An element of the shortage crisis is the willingness of superintendents to move to other districts, and how often they move, giving a sense of their willingness to enter the "job market" and their longevity in the position. We assessed mobility in five related ways. First, we asked respondents how willing they were to take a "good" job in another district, should one appear? Second, using years in respondents' current and "previous" positions to get some sense of job longevity and movement, we asked how many years superintendents had served in their current posts? Third, we asked what types of jobs they might consider and how strongly attracted they were to such posts? Fourth, we asked what general and particular (technical) skills respondents believed they could bring to these new positions? And fifth, given these responses, to what types of districts were they particularly attracted? Together, these measures give a real sense of how, where, and under what circumstances current superintendents would consider working in new locations and types of districts.

- *Would you take a "good" job in another district?* _____

SPEAR™ asked superintendents, "If a 'good' job opened up in another district, would you take the job if offered?" Table 3 shows the responses to this critical question, to which about half of respondents answered "Yes."

- **Mobility by District Size:** Most mobile were the leaders of the smallest districts, with 14.9 percent responding "Yes, Definitely" and 40.6 percent indicating "Yes, maybe" they would take a good job in another district. Least willing to consider a new post were leaders of the nation's largest systems, with 34.9 percent saying "Yes," but only 11.6 percent responding "Yes, Definitely."

Table 3
Job Mobility of School Superintendents
(N=1,687)

	All Superintendents (N=1,687) Frequency %	Large Districts (n=86) Frequency %	Medium Districts (n=1,025) Frequency %	Small Districts (n=576) Frequency %
"Yes-Definitely Take Job"	232 (13.8%)	10 (11.6%)	136 (13.3%)	86 (14.9%)
"Yes, Maybe"	628 (37.2%)	30 (34.9%)	364 (35.5%)	234 (40.6%)
TOTAL "Yes's"	**860 (51.0%)**	**40 (46.5%)**	**500 (48.8%)**	**320 (55.5%)**
"Probably NO"	553 (32.8%)	29 (33.7%)	351 (34.2%)	173 (30.0%)
"Definitely NO"	274 (16.2%)	17 (19.8%)	174 (17.0%)	83 (14.5%)
TOTAL "No's"	**827 (49.0%)**	**46 (53.5%)**	**525 (51.2%)**	**256 (44.5%)**
Overall TOTAL	1,687 (100.0%)	86 (100.0%)	1,025 (100.0%)	576 (100.0%)

Overall, however, 49 percent of those surveyed said "No—they would definitely or probably NOT move." When analyzed by district size, 53.5 percent of superintendents from large districts, 51.2 percent from medium size districts, and 44.5 percent of those from small districts indicated an unwillingness to consider changing jobs. Some observers might be surprised that about half the incumbent superintendents would even consider moving (although only 14 percent said "Yes, Definitely") to another "good" job.

• **Mobility by Region:** We aggregated superintendents' mobility by the 10 standard regions of the country using U.S. Census Bureau categories to determine whether superintendents in certain parts of the country indicate a greater willingness to relocate than those in other regions (See Table 4).

Table 4
Superintendents' Mobility Rank-Ordered by Regions

CENSUS REGIONS:	Mean	"Total Yes" Freq. %	"Total No" Freq. %
West South Central (n=112)	2.34	72 (64.3%)	40 (35.7%)
Mountain (n=107)	2.48	58 (54.2%)	49 (45.8%)
West North Central (n=241)	2.42	130 (53.9%)	111 (46.1%)
South Atlantic (n=156)	2.48	83 (53.2%)	73 (46.8%)
East North Central (n=390)	2.54	191 (49.0%)	199 (51.0%)
Mid-Atlantic (n=301)	2.49	155 (50.8%)	148 (49.2%)
Pacific (n=173)	2.62	81 (46.8%)	92 (53.2%)
New England (n=99)	2.65	43 (43.4%)	56 (56.6%)
East South Central (n=64)	2.22	25 (39.2%)	39 (60.8%)
All Regions (n=1,687)	2.52	860 (51.0%)	827 (49.0%)

As shown in Table 4 (column 2), superintendents in the *West South Central* area (AK, LA, TX, and OK) indicated the greatest willingness to relocate; 64.3 percent said they would definitely or probably take a new job if offered. In contrast, respondents from the *East South Central* states (KY, MI, TN, AL, MS, OH, IN, IL, MO, WI) indicated the least willingness, with only 39.2% indicating a willingness to relocate. The superintendents from *New England* states (ME, VT, NH, MA, RI, and CT) appeared also uninterested in moving, with only 43.4% indicating a willingness to relocate.

Thus, only about half the superintendents in this survey indicated any interest in relocating to another part of the country. Some might say that, given the pressures of the job and the lack of incentives, even half is a significant number of "mobile superintendents"; others might say that this is not a very active labor pool for America's schools.

Years in current and previous jobs? _____

SPEAR™ also looked at just how mobile the superintendents have been to date. We gathered longevity data for each respondent's current superintendency, as well as where they served previously, and for how long. This information indicates something about their job stability and their ascent "up the ladder." As shown in Table 5, the average years of service in their current district for all respondents is 7.25 years, and the average for previous positions is 6.43 years. These findings cast some doubt on the usual arguments that superintendents only last about 3 years, Renchler (1992) found the national average tenure of superintendents was 5.6 years.

As seen in Table 5, respondents from large districts have been in place the shortest number of years, with medium and small district superintendents in place for longer periods, respectively. Interestingly, respondents' time in their previous posts is very similar, regardless of current district size.

Table 5 also looks at the total number of years respondents spent holding central-office, school building administrator, and classroom positions. Again, while the literature on the superintendency seems to indicate a highly mobile population, our data show superintendents to be a seasoned, highly experienced cohort of education administrators, with 30 years of experience: 15.3 years working in the central office, 7.79 years at the building administrator level, and 6.91 years in the classroom.

Table 5
Superintendents' Career Mobility:
Years in Current and Past Positions

	All Supts.	Large Districts	Medium Districts	Small Districts
Longevity	Mean	Mean	Mean	Mean
Current Post	7.25	4.71	7.28	7.63
Previous Post	6.43	6.49	6.45	6.43
Total Current/Previous	13.68	11.20	13.73	14.06
Job Locations/Yrs.	Mean	Mean	Mean	Mean
YEARS in *Central Office* Admin.	15.30	16.5	16.53	2.77
YEARS in *School* Admin.	7.79	7.14	7.19	9.06
YEARS in *Classroom*	6.91	6.14	6.46	7.82
TOTAL YEARS in EDUCATION	30.0 yrs.	29.78 yrs.	30.18 yrs.	29.65 yrs.

The average career path for superintendents in our study was as a teacher for just less than 7 years, a principal for less than 8 years, followed by 15 years in the central office, including the current post. However, the pattern in the small, less populous, and often rural districts is slightly different than the "fast track" for larger systems: small district superintendents were teachers almost a year, on average, longer than their medium (6.46 years) and large district counterparts, with those from large district spending the least time in the classroom at 6.14 years.

The large district superintendents in our study also served the least time as building level administrators, at 7.14 years, compared to medium district superintendents at 7.19 years and those from small districts, at 9.06 years. Overall, big system administrators in our study were promoted up the hierarchy more quickly (perhaps more opportunity for positions), spending less time in the classroom as teachers and school building as principals.

What type of district would you consider for the next job? _____

SPEAR^{TM} also looked at what types of districts (rural, large urban, suburban, inner-city, and "same as current location") the superintendents find most attractive by asking them to rate district types on a four-point scale. Since we grouped the districts by size, we can tell to what degree superintendents stay within the general size and type where they currently work, or whether, for example, a rural superintendent would positively consider an inner-city district.

Table 6 gives the mean scores and frequencies for attractiveness of locations for all superintendents and by district size. To make the data a bit more manageable, we combined the No and Low Attraction scores and the Moderate and High Attraction scores into two categories, No/Low and Moderate/High.

Table 6
Location Preferences for Superintendent Mobility

TYPE:	All Districts	Large	Medium	Small
RURAL				
Mean	1.60	.62	1.31	2.21
No/Low	711 (44.0%)	68 (86.1%)	521 (53.7%)	122 (21.5%)
Mod/High	905 (56.0%)	11 (13.9%)	448 (46.3%)	446 (78.5%)
TOTAL	1,616 (100%)	79 (100.0%)	969 (100.0%)	568 (100.0%)
Large Urban				
Mean	0.98	2.33	1.07	.60
No/Low	1,121 (69.0%)	14 (16.1%)	639 (65.5%)	468 (83.3%)
Mod/High	504 (31.0%)	73 (83.9%)	337 (34.5%)	94 (16.7%)
TOTAL	1,625 (100%)	87 (100%)	976 (100%)	562 (100%)
Suburban				
Mean	2.42	2.22	2.61	2.11
No/Low	206 (12.4%)	16 (18.8%)	62 (6.2%)	128 (22.5%)
Mod/High	1,460 (87.6%)	69 (81.2%)	950 (93.8%)	441 (77.5%)
TOTAL	1,666 (100%)	85 (100%)	1,012 (100%)	569 (100%)
Inner-City				
Mean	.64	1.68	.72	.37
No/Low	1,304 (81.7%)	33 (40.7%)	758 (79.2%)	513 (91.8%)
Mod/High	293 (18.3%)	48 (59.3%)	199 (20.8%)	46 (8.2%)
TOTAL	1,597 (100%)	81 (100%)	957 (100%)	559 (100%)
Similar to Now				
Mean	2.62	2.66	2.65	2.56
No/Low	119 (7.1%)	6 (7.1%)	59 (5.8%)	54 (9.5%)
Mod/High	1,537 (92.9%)	79 (92.9%)	940 (94.2%)	518 (90.5%)
TOTAL	1,656 (100%)	85 (100%)	999 (100%)	572 (100%)

The majority of superintendents were most attracted to the type of district in which they currently work, with 92.9 percent indicating they would like to work in a district "similar to the one where they now work." Overall, superintendents were most attracted to *suburban* districts, followed by *rural* districts. *Inner-city* districts were the least attractive overall, with 81.7 percent of respondents indicating "Low or No" attraction to them. *Large urban* districts, likewise, were among the least attractive, with only 31 percent of respondents finding them moderately or highly attractive.

We know that suburban systems come in all sizes and with a range of racial, social, and economic differences. We also know that the United States now has more suburban (metropolitan area) districts than larger, urban or small rural districts. Furthermore, we know from our data on service in the central office that many superintendents "wait their turn." Large, urban, and inner-city districts tend to either hire "from within" or select leaders from other big cities. Thus, the market is segmented by type and size. As long as leaders from within school district types are willing to apply for jobs, the flow should be maintained (see Kowalski, 1995). However, if the nation continues to see a shortage of candidates within these various types of districts, it may be difficult in some locations to recruit across types (rural to urban, urban to rural, suburban to rural or urban). The data show the danger inherent in treating the superintendency market as unitary or uni-dimensional.

What skills do superintendents bring to their job? _____

Mobility is undoubtedly related to the skill sets and interests that superintendents recognize and possess, and that hiring school boards require. Early research on "executive succession" among superintendents found that certain highly mobile superintendents were called "hoppers" (see Carlson, 1966). These superintendents had special skills and moved from district to district, depending upon where their specialty was in demand. For example, a superintendent might be known as a "facilities person," showing the ability to get bond issues drafted and passed, architects set to work, and construction completed on new school buildings. In a joking manner, one such leader explained that he had a chronic case of the "edifice complex." Once construction stops and the district no longer needs a "builder," the "facilities" superintendent moves on to another district undertaking school construction.

The *SPEAR* questionnaire looked at the following sub-specialties: Building Construction/Bond Issues, Human Relations, Labor Relations, Race Relations, Curriculum Design, Staff Development, Community Relations, Finance/Budgeting, and Technology. Respondents were asked to indicate High Expertise=3, Moderate Expertise=2, Low Expertise=1, and No Expertise=0, giving us some sense of their perceived job skills and strengths.

Table 7 shows the various skill sets superintendents believe they bring to their positions. Looking at the table, we see several interesting, but not entirely unexpected, patterns emerge.

• **People Skills:** First, superintendents appear to be "people people," with strong skills in the interpersonal areas of *Human Relations* and *Community Relations.* For *Human Relations,* for example, 99.5 percent of superintendents indicated that they possess "High/Moderate" skills. This trend held across all district sizes. The abilities to work with people, communicate, and relate to communities are the "survival skills" of the superintendencies.

Table 7
Skills of Superintendents

SKILLS:	All Districts	Large	Medium	Small
Construction/ Bond Issues				
Mean	2.39	2.38	2.45	2.28
No/Low	180 (10.6%)	9 (10.2%)	90 (8.7%)	81 (14.1%)
Mod/High	1,520 (89.4%)	79 (89.8%)	941 (91.3%)	500 (85.9%)
TOTAL	1,700 (100%)	88 (100.0%)	1,031 (100%)	581 (100%)
Human Relations				
Mean	2.84	2.90	2.84	2.83
No/Low	8 (0.5%)	0 (0%)	5 (0.5%)	3 (0.5%)
Mod/High	1,699 (99.5%)	88 (100%)	1,032 (99.5%)	579 (99.5%)
TOTAL	1,707 (100%)	88 (100%)	1,037 (100%)	582 (100%)
Labor Relations				
Mean	2.38	2.36	2.37	2.40
No/Low	209 (12.3%)	10 (11.4%)	133 (12.8%)	66 (11.3%)
Mod/High	1,495 (87.7%)	78 (88.6%)	901 (87.2%)	516 (88.7%)
TOTAL	1,704 (100%)	88 (100%)	1,034 (100%)	582 (100%)
Race Relations				
Mean	1.85	2.51	1.95	1.58
No/Low	596 (35.0%)	5 (5.7%)	300 (29.1%)	291 (50.0%)
Mod/High	1,107 (65.0%)	83 (94.3%)	733 (70.9%)	291 (50.0%)
TOTAL	1,703 (100%)	88 (100%)	1,033 (100%)	582 (100%)
Management SKILLS:	All Districts	Large	Medium	Small

Curriculum Design				
Mean	2.36	2.49	2.42	2.24
No/Low	129 (7.7%)	4 (4.5%)	57 (5.5%)	68 (11.7%)
Mod/High	1,576 (92.3%)	84 (95.5%)	976 (94.5%)	516 (88.3%)
TOTAL	1,705 (100%)	88 (100%)	1,033 (100%)	584 (100%)
Staff Development				
Mean	2.48	2.52	2.50	2.45
No/Low	53 (3.1%)	2 (2.3%)	25 (2.4%)	26 (4.4%)
Mod/High	1,654 (96.9%)	86 (97.7%)	1,009 (97.6%)	559 (95.6%)
TOTAL	1,707 (100%)	88 (100%)	1,034 (100%)	585 (100%)
Community Relations				
Mean	2.79	2.90	2.82	2.72
No/Low	5 (.3%)	0 (0%)	2 (0.2%)	3 (0.5%)
Mod/High	1,702 (99.7%)	88 (100%)	1,034 (99.8%)	580 (99.5%)
TOTAL	1,707 (100%)	88 (100%)	1,036 (100%)	583 (100%)
Finance/Budget				
Mean	2.58	2.44	2.57	2.63
No/Low	45 (2.6%)	4	26	15 (2.6%)
Mod/High	1,662 (97.4%)	84 (95.5%)	1,008 (97.5%)	570 (97.4%)
TOTAL	1,707 (100%)	88 (100%)	1,034 (100%)	585 (100%)
Technology				
Mean (SD)	2.19	2.00	2.17	2.25
No/Low	231 (13.5%)	20 (22.7%)	140 (13.7%)	71 (12.3%)
Mod/High	1,569 (86.5%)	68 (77.3%)	892 (86.3%)	509 (87.7%)
TOTAL	1,700 (100%)	88 (100%)	1,032 (100%)	580 (100%)

Community Relations, a skill that includes working with school board members and other key community groups, also ranked high on superintendents' lists of their skills. Almost all, 99.7 percent, respondents believe they possess moderate/high skills in this area.

• **Areas of Expertise:** Next, we looked at skills that seem more technical and specific: Finance and Budgeting, Staff Development, Construction, Labor Relations, and Curriculum Design. Respondents' reported expertise level in these areas, while still high overall, is lower than in the more universal categories of human and community relations.

Of the respondents, 97.4 percent indicated that they possess skills in finance and budgeting; 96.9 percent indicated skills in staff development. Interestingly, less than 90 percent indicated expertise in school construction/bond issues or labor relations. A larger percentage (92.3) indicated expertise in curriculum design, suggesting the importance of superintendents as instructional leaders.

• **Specialized Skills:** We also asked about Race Relations and Education Technology, which we consider specialized areas of expertise. On these, we see strong but somewhat lower scores, probably indicating that superintendents oversee but do not always handle these areas directly themselves.

Technology is the newcomer to the list of skills superintendents must master. The arrival of e-rate government subsidies, dozens of new computers and software packages, and the need to use and teach "technology" indicates the importance of this area. Yet, our data show that superintendents feel less expert in the area of technology than other areas. This may reflect the fact that our average respondent is in his or her 50s, with 30 years in education.

Ranking lowest among the 11 skills areas, *Race Relations* was most germane to school systems with large immigrant, African-American, and Latino communities. As we might expect, the overall skill rating of superintendents was the lowest for this of the nine areas in our survey.

Differences by Gender?

• **Superintendents' Gender:** Table 8 indicates that only l2.2 percent of the sample superintendents were women. In the large districts, however, the percent was considerably higher, with 20 out of 88, or 22.7 percent women. Some of the literature indicates that minority women have a better opportunity to attain the top spot in the large school districts (see Jackson, 1995; Casserly, 1992; Glass, 1992), although other researchers such as Ornstein (1992) have found that women are no more likely to reach the top spot in a large district than in any other size system.

Table 8
Gender of Sample Superintendents
(N=1,712)

	All Supts.	Large Districts	Medium Districts	Small Districts
Male	1,503 (87.8%)	68 (77.3%)	908 (87.5%)	527 (89.9%)
Female	209 (12.2%)	20 (22.7%)	130 (12.5%)	59 (10.1%)
TOTAL	1,712 (100%)	88 (100%)	1,038 (100%)	586 (100%)

We compared male and female superintendents along five key dimensions of this study: (1) their *longevity* in current and previous positions; (2) their prior years of *experience* in the classroom, school, and central office; (3) their *satisfaction* with their work; (4) the *attractiveness* of jobs by location and type; and (5) the skills and *expertise* they believe they bring to the job. Tables 9 and 10 present the findings of these five dimensions.

• **Longevity and Experience:** Data show that male superintendents have served in current and past positions significantly longer than female superintendents: 7.57 years in current and 6.54 years in past jobs, compared to women leaders with 5.01 and 5.66 years.

Table 9 (rows 3-5) compares years of professional experience in the classroom, school, and central office for superintendents by gender. It shows that female superintendents tended to remain in *classroom teaching* significantly longer (8.99 years) than their male counterparts (6.62 years). Conversely, however, the men in our study spent more years at the *building level* (8.02 years) than the women (5.98 years). And years in the *central office* were also significantly different by gender, with men at 15.62 total years and women 12.99 years.

These findings show that both men and women "move up the ladder" rather quickly, leaving the classroom and building-level administration to assume central-office posts in rather short order. Interestingly, the data indicate that the average male superintendent spends more years in the central office (15.62 years) than at the classroom and school level (14.64 years), while female superintendents spend more years teaching and in building-level administration (14.97 years) than in the central office (12.99 years).

• **Job Satisfaction:** Table 9 (rows 6 and 7) compares job satisfaction with "curricular work" and "making a difference for kids" by gender. In both cases, female superintendents had slightly more positive responses on 5-point Likert scale: 4.3 for female superintendents, compared to 4.1 for males. Similarly, in "making a difference for students," females averaged 4.8 out of 5.0, and male superintendents 4.7. Thus, both groups gained a sense of satisfaction and accomplishment around the kids and the curriculum; although women slightly but significantly more so.

Table 9: Characteristics and Attitudes of Superintendents *by Gender*

Variable Number And Name:	Supts.' Gender	Number of Cases (N)	Mean Score
LONGEVITY			
1. Longevity: Yrs. In Current Job	Male: Female:	1,504 208	7.57 yrs. 5.01 yrs.
2. Longevity: Yrs. In Previous Post	Male: Female:	1,489 207	6.54 yrs. 5.66 yrs.
EXPERIENCE			
3. Experience: Yrs. in the Classroom	Male: Female:	1,493 206	6.62 yrs. 8.99 yrs.
4. Experience: Yrs. In School-Site Admin.	Male: Female:	1,437 190	8.02 yrs. 5.98 yrs.
5. Experience: Yrs. in Central Office	Male: Female:	1,467 205	15.62 yrs. 12.99 yrs.
SATISFACTION			**(1-5 scale)**
6. Satisfaction: With Curricular Work	Male: Female:	1,501 204	4.122 4.335
7. Satisfaction: Making a difference for kids	Male: Female:	1,500 209	4.665 4.804
JOB ATTRACTION			
8. Attraction: to Rural District	Male: Female:	1,418 198	1.645 1.301
9. Attraction: to Large Urban District	Male: Female:	1,425 198	.948 1.171
10. Attraction: to Inner-city District	Male: Female:	1,399 196	.6019 .9184

• **Attraction to Districts by Type:** We also checked to see if women superintendents are attracted to jobs in different district types than men. As shown in Table 9, rows 8-10, men were weakly but significantly more attracted to rural districts than women. While neither group was strongly attracted to large/urban and inner-city districts, women were slightly more attracted than men. Both groups preferred suburban at 2.42 out of 3.0, with no significant differences by gender.

• **Job Expertise:** We were curious whether male and female superintendents differed significantly in their personal perceptions of the level of skill they bring to the job in the different areas in our study. As shown in Table 10, rows 11-14, some differences do exist. Males indicated 2.41 out of 3.0 on Building Construction and Bond Issue skills (facilities planning) while females were also high at 2.19 but significantly below males. In Race Relations, Curriculum Design, and Staff Development skills, however, female superintendents' ratings were significantly higher than those reported by the males. The finding for race relations seems consistent with the fact that female superintendents were also slightly more interested in the inner-city systems.

Table 10: Superintendents' Interest Areas by Gender

Variable Number And Name:	Supts.' Gender	Number of Cases (N)	Mean Score	Degrees of Freedom
EXPERTISE: 1. Job Expertise: Construction/Bonds	Male: Female:	1,494 205	2.4137 2.1902	1697
2. Job Expertise: Race Relations	Male: Female:	1,496 206	1.8189 2.0583	1700
3. Job Expertise: Curriculum Design	Male: Female:	1,499 206	2.3106 2.7136	1701
4. Job Expertise: Staff Development	Male: Female:	1,499 206	2.4390 2.7816	1703

Membership in Superintendent Organizations? _____

Another focus of the *SPEAR*[TM] survey was to determine the level of participation of U.S. superintendents in national and state school management associations. We asked respondents to indicate whether they were members of the American Association of School Administrators (AASA), the national superintendents' group; members of their state AASA; both; or neither. Table

11 shows the incredible networking of this random sample of the nation's school superintendents. Nearly two-thirds (65.2%) are members of *both* AASA and their state affiliates, with medium-sized district leaders at 66.5 percent, small at 64.7 percent, and large at the lowest level, 51.7 percent.

When we separate AASA and the state associations from "both," we see that only 1.2 percent of the 87 large district superintendents are members of neither – and a high percentage (43.7%) are affiliated with national AASA but not the state affiliate. This difference may reflect the fact that leaders of larger districts tend to look to other districts of similar size and type, rather than to networks made up of the smaller systems within their states.

Most impressive is that out of 1,702 school executives responding to this survey item, only 15 (or 0.9 percent) are not affiliated with state, national, or both associations. We can conclude from this finding that the nation's top education leaders seem to affiliate with other superintendents through state and national AASA. This networking assists in building reputations, supporting egos, and increasing mobility.

Table 11
Superintendent Membership in
National and State Associations

Association AFFILIATION	ALL Districts Freq. %	Large Districts Freq. %	Medium Districts Freq. %	Small Districts Freq. %
Both AASA and State Supts.' Association	1,109 (65.2%)	45 (51.7%)	686 (66.5%)	378 (64.7%)
AASA Member Only	540 (31.7%)	38 (43.7%)	316 (30.7%)	186 (31.8%)
State Association Only	38 (2.2%)	3 (3.4%)	18 (1.7%)	17 (2.9%)
No Affiliation: State or National	15 (.9%)	1 (1.2%)	11 (1.1%)	3 (.6)
Total:	1,702 (100%)	87 (100%)	1,031 (100%)	584 (100%)

Pensions_____

Pensions are another issue in superintendents' decisions about moving to other positions, within their state or outside it. Given that nearly 80 percent (79.1%) of our sample are in their 50s and 60s (68.4 percent between 50 and 59 years of age; 10.7%, sixty or more), the vesting and retirement process is a critical element in whether and where superintendents continue to work.

Table 12 presents the distribution of ages for the superintendents in this study. Because respondents sometimes balk at reporting their age, we found it easier to ask them to put themselves in a "decade." We got good responses, with 1,713 providing their age decade on *SPEAR™*.

Table 12
Distribution of Age Cohorts

Age Cohorts:	All Supts. Freq. %	Large Districts Freq. %	Medium Districts Freq. %	Small Districts Freq. %
20-29 yrs.	2 (0.1%)	0 (0%)	1 (0.1%)	1 (0.2%)
30-39 yrs.	10 (0.6%)	0 (0%)	2 (0.2%)	8 (1.4%)
40-49 yrs.	344 (20.2%)	16 (18.2%)	177 (17.0%)	151 (25.8%)
50-59 yrs.	1,173 (68.4%)	58 (65.9%)	747 (71.9%)	368 (62.8%)
60-plus yrs.	184 (10.7%)	14 (15.9%)	112 (10.8%)	58 (9.8%)
Total:	1,713 (100%)	88 (100%)	1,039 (100%)	586 (100%)

As expected, very few respondents are under 40 years of age: only 12 or under 1 percent (0.7%). Slightly more than 20 percent are in their 40s overall. We see greater numbers of "younger" leaders in the small systems (25.8 percent are between 40 and 49 years of age), while only 18.2 percent are in that age span in large districts and 17 percent in medium sized districts. Hence, it appears that small districts might offer initial opportunities to younger candidates for the superintendency.

As we said, the majority of superintendents in our study (68.4 percent) are in the 50-59 years age range. Large districts have the most members of the 60-plus age group at 15.9 percent, medium districts have 10.8 percent, while small districts have only 9.8 percent.

Given this age distribution, it is clear why pensions and retirement are critical issues for superintendents. Unlike university professors who "take their pensions with them" across state lines, K-12 educators are members of a retirement program specific to the state in which they work. (For a full discussion of the issue of "non-portability" of state education retirement programs, see Auriemma, Cooper and Smith, 1991.)

Superintendents in this survey were asked whether they were currently vested in their state pension program. Given that the mean years in education for superintendents is about 30, unless a superintendent took a job in another state, most would be vested. Table 13 shows the data and confirms that, overall, 86.2 percent of our sample superintendents are fully vested in a retirement program. In most states, vesting occurs after about 5 years of service, meaning that an educator who leaves the state after 5 years (vesting) can reclaim both their pension contribution and whatever financial contributions the district and state have made.

Table 13
Current Pension Vesting Status of Sample Superintendents
By District Size (N=1,703)

	All Supts.	Large Districts	Medium Districts	Small Districts
Yes, Vested	1,468 (86.2%)	66 (75.9%)	890 (86.0%)	512 (88.1%)
Not Vested	235 (13.8%)	21 (24.1%)	145 (14.0%)	69 (11.9%)
TOTAL	1,703 (100%)	87 (100%)	1,035 (100%)	581 (100%)

When presented by district size, we see that of the large district superintendents, only 75.9 are vested, presumably because of their tendency to move across state lines, compared to 88.1 percent in small districts and 86.0 percent in medium sized systems.

We also asked respondents to indicate the number of states in which they are vested -- an indicator of previous job mobility. As shown in Table 14, most superintendents (80.3 percent) are vested in a single state, showing a tendency during their 30 or more years to remain in one state for their careers and thus to build a pension in that state's retirement program. However, 15.3 percent are vested in two states, 1.9 percent in three, and .1 percent in four states.

Table 14
Vesting by Number of States for Superintendents
(N=1,609)

	All Supts.	Large Districts	Medium Districts	Small Districts
0 States	39 (2.4%)	4 (4.9%)	19 (1.9%)	16 (2.9%)
1 State	1,292 (80.3%)	52 (64.2%)	764 (78.1%)	476 (86.6%)
2 States	246 (15.3%)	23 (28.4%)	169 (17.3%)	54 (9.8%)
3 States	31 (1.9%)	2 (2.5%)	25 (2.6%)	4 (0.7%)
4 States	1 (.1%)	0 (0%)	1 (0.1%)	0 (0%)
TOTAL:	1,609 (100%)	81 (100%)	978 (100%)	550 (100%)

Finally, we asked respondents on *SPEAR*^{TM} who were vested in more than one state whether they would consider returning to the other state where they were already vested. As shown in Table 15, overall, 67 percent indicated that "Yes," they would return to the state to take advantage of their vested status.

In the large districts, the percentage was highest at 72.2 percent; medium districts were next at 67.8 percent; and small were lowest at 64.1 percent. Again, small district leaders appeared least willing to be mobile, given the smaller percentage. Whatever the levels of vesting in a pension scheme, data do seem to indicate the importance of pensions in the mobility of superintendents, at least across states.

Table 15
Superintendents' Willingness to Return
to Another State if Vested There
(N=816)

	All Supts.	Large Districts	Medium Districts	Small Districts
Yes, Would Return	547 (67.0%)	39 (72.2%)	356 (67.8%)	152 (64.1%)
No, Would Not Return	269 (33.0%)	15 (27.8%)	169 (32.2%)	85 (35.9%)
TOTAL:	816 (100%)	54 (100%)	525 (100%)	237 (100%)

Academic Degrees

A high percentage of respondents to the *SPEAR*^{TM} survey have earned doctorates (a Ph.D. or Ed.D.).

• **Superintendents' Earned Degrees:** Table 16 shows that 64.2 percent of incumbent superintendents hold a doctoral degree. In the large districts, 79.3 percent hold an Ed.D. or Ph.D., while 75.1 percent of medium sized district leaders have doctorates, and a much lower percentage (43.3) in the small systems. As for other degrees, Table 16 shows that 30.8 percent of our sample have a master's plus extra credits; 1.3 percent a MA/MS degree and no additional credits; and less than one percent (.6%) have a BA/BS alone. Some 2.9 percent have "Other" degrees, such as MBAs or law degrees. Masters-plus graduate credits was highest in the small systems at 47.6 percent (the predominant degree there).

The relatively low percentage of doctorates in small systems may indicate that school boards in rural and smaller communities do not expect to find doctorates and may promote others with lesser training regionally or internally. No respondents from the large districts had only a BA/BS or master's degree; all had a doctorate, master's-plus, or some other professional degree.

Table 16
Highest Degree Awarded for Sample Superintendents
(N=1,712)

	All Supts.	Large Districts	Medium Districts	Small Districts
Doctorate	1,102 (64.2%)	69 (79.3%)	779 (75.1%)	254 (43.3%)
Masters-Plus	528 (30.8%)	17 (19.5%)	231 (22.2%)	280 (47.6%)
MA/MS	23 (1.3%)	0 (0%)	5 (0.5%)	18 (3.1%)
BA/BS	10 (0.6%)	0 (0%)	5 (0.5%)	5 (0.9%)
Other	49 (2.9%)	1 (1.2%)	18 (1.7%)	30 (5.1%)
TOTAL	1,712 (100%)	87 (100%)	1,038 (100%)	587 (100%)

Incentives Driving Superintendents as Professionals? _____

The *SPEAR*^TM survey presented a series of statements about the role and career of the superintendent, asking incumbents to indicate their reactions on a scale of 5 ("Strongly Agree") to 1 ("Strongly Disagree"). These sub-scales and items were designed to elicit a sense from those surveyed about how they view the (1) *economics* of being a superintendent; (2) level of *career satisfaction* they get from their work; (3) *personal incentives* emerging from their work; (4) *familial* concerns related to job mobility; and (5) *job organization* of the superintendency.

• **Economic Incentives:** Five items were explored under the heading of economics of the job, including pay levels, perks (funds for house, car, travel), higher cost of moving to another district, capping of raises, and low pay differentials when compared with the earnings of other educators.

As shown in Table 17, as a cluster of items (a sub-scale), the overall mean for Economic Incentives was 3.75, with these items being of greatest concern in the small districts. Of all the economic items, interestingly, "low pay" was the least salient (mean=3.46); few perks was next at 3.59; the cost of living involved with a move was next at 3.63.

It appears that economic concerns are on the minds of superintendents, particularly concerns related to the inability to get a "decent" raise (capping policies) and the relative pay levels of superintendents when compared to teachers and principals.

• **Career Satisfaction:** We asked superintendents to indicate what satisfied them about their careers as education executives and whether they would advise others to enter the profession. This sub-scale took the long view, a chance for reflection on what satisfied school leaders. As shown in Table 17, the overall mean for satisfaction was 3.80, yet certain individual items of the sub-scale were considerably higher, depending on "what" the superintendents were satisfied with.

Interestingly, as district size declined, so did the levels of job satisfaction. Satisfaction levels for superintendents working in larger districts averaged 3.93 out of a possible 5.0.; in medium-sized districts, 3.86; and those responding in the smallest systems, 3.69. It is hard to explain the drop across size categories. Perhaps smaller systems are demanding and superintendents do not have the system scale or resources to hire assistants to build a team. Or perhaps working in a "friends and neighbors" atmosphere, where everyone is someone's cousin or aunt, limits the professional latitude of small district leaders. Perhaps, the example of the decline of the small town doctor is analogous, as physicians want to work in metropolitan areas where they can have stimulation, colleagues, and a chance to escape the constant scrutiny of small town America.

Table 17
Incentives and Disincentives for Superintendents' Careers and Mobility

	All Supts. Mean	Large Districts Mean	Medium Districts Mean	Small Districts Mean
1. Economic Concerns	3.75	3.56	3.70	3.85
2. Career Satisfaction	3.80	3.93	3.86	3.69
3. Personal Incentives	3.86	3.91	3.89	3.78
4. Family Concerns	3.13	3.05	3.13	3.14
5. Job Organization	3.96	2.97	3.96	3.98
6. Recruitment Incentives	4.07	4.07	4.04	4.12

So, given all the stress and strain, would a superintendent recommend the job to others? And, when all is said and done, is the career a satisfying one? We offered these items in the instrument:

SPEAR™ Item: *"In advising fellow educators, I would truly recommend the profession of superintendent of schools as a meaningful, satisfying career."*

Response: Data show a moderate but strong, positive response to this item, 3.74, meaning that superintendents would recommend the job to others.

Item: *"My work in this district has given me real career satisfaction."*

Response: The mean score 4.47, between "Agree Strongly" (5) and "Agree Somewhat" (4), makes it clear that, despite all the pressures and problems, America's school superintendents express real satisfaction with their careers.

• **Personal Incentives to Pursue the Superintendency:** The **SPEAR**™ survey also isolated areas of potential concern to superintendents, including their family, the organization and structure of the job, and the economics of the job. We included a series of personal items to test the salience of this dimension of why school executives might enter or leave the profession, move to a new job, or stay put.

Item: *"I was personally motivated in my decision to become a superintendent by the authority and status associated with the job."* Response: Mean score for all 1,719 superintendents on this item was low at 3.09 out of 5.0, indicating that school executives understand the limits on their power and do not take the job because of either power, authority, or prestige. So, why do they seek the work?

Item: *"The opportunity to make a significant difference in the lives of children was a strong personal incentive for my becoming a superintendent."* Response: The average rating on this item was the highest on the entire survey: 4.68 out of 5.0, showing high consensus that helping kids, which is at the very heart of the mission of education, is a prime motivator for superintendents.

The overall sub-score for Personal Incentives, as shown in Table 17, line 3, was 3.86, which includes a range of incentives, such as power, authority, risks, as well as the needs of students.

• **Familial Concerns:** One might assume that a leader's willingness to consider job mobility would be affected by the necessity to uproot the family, sell the house, force the spouse to find another job (if the new post is too far away to commute), and give up neighbors and friends, not to mention relatives. As shown in Table 17, the mean on a 5-point Likert scale seems moderate at 3.13. It appears to be slightly less of an issue for large system leaders at 3.05 compared to 3.13 and 3.14 for respondents from moderate and small systems, respectively. Take for example:

Item: *"Moving my family is a problem for me when applying for new superintendent jobs in other regions."* Response: Mean of 2.31. Perhaps, given the age of superintendents today, most have already finished raising their children, so moving may be less of a problem than anticipated.

• **Job Organization Issues:** Much of the literature on the superintendency mentions the structure of the job and relations with key political groups, such as the school board, as critical factors in considering a career move. Our survey confirms both of these assertions, but one stands out over the other.

SPEAR™ Item: *"The job organization of the superintendent is too demanding of time and energy to attract new and talented candidates to the position."* Response: Mean for this item was 3.61, showing moderate agreement.

Item: *"My relationship with the school board is critical to me in making important education decisions."* Response: Average of 4.66, meaning very strong agreement. Superintendents learn early and often that their relationship with the board of education is critical to the job. Overall, as shown in Table 17, the mean sub-score for all the Job Organization items was 3.96. Structure, relationship, decision-making -- the whole process of governing and managing -- remain of concern to the nation's superintendents.

What Do Superintendents Want? _____

We asked superintendents about practical steps states, school boards, and other public agencies could take to make the job more attractive and rewarding, and thus to increase the size of the applicant pool. SPEAR™ offered six options, including (a) tenure for superintendents, (b) higher pay, (c) better perks such as housing and car allowances, (d) more help from the district, (e) more support from universities, and (f) recognition and rewards from professional associations such as AASA. When these solutions are compared, we see that superintendents most support higher pay and more help from the district.

Item: *"Higher pay and better benefits would bring more candidates into the applicant pool."* Out of a possible 5.0 ("Strongly Agree"), the overall respondent mean was 4.43, with the small district leaders indicating the highest positive response at 4.52, large district leaders next at 4.41, and medium sized districts leaders at 4.38. In the eyes of incumbent superintendents, the pay and benefit package is a way to bring new talent into the applicant pool. Ranking very close to the economic incentive, however, is more help from the district

Item: *"Districts should consider giving current superintendents more help and support to ensure their well-being and job success."* Overall, the mean was a high 4.42; the response was even higher for superintendents from the large districts at 4.48; 4.39 for superintendents in medium sized systems; and an average of 4.48 for superintendents in the small school systems.

In the middle of the distribution come three additional steps that our superintendents think will improve the flow of candidates: *better perks*, such as financial help with housing, cars, and professional meetings, with an overall mean of 4.19; *recognition from professional associations*, at 4.08; and *assistance from universities and other institutions*, with an overall average of 3.93.

Surprisingly, *tenure for superintendents* was the least attractive step to improve the nature of the job, with an overall mean of 3.39. However, a rather high Standard Deviation of 1.25 for the tenure item indicates wide disagreement. A small minority of superintendents "Agreed Strongly" with the need for superintendent tenure, creating some divergence of opinion on this controversial idea.

Table 18
Superintendents' Attitudes Toward
Practical Steps to Enhance their Jobs

	All Supts. (N=1,633) Mean	Large Districts (n=83) Mean	Medium Districts (n=964) Mean	Small Districts (n=586) Mean
1. Tenure for Superintendents	3.39	3.19	3.32	3.54
2. Higher Pay for Superintendents	4.43	4.41	4.38	4.52
3. Better Perks for Superintendents	4.19	4.21	4.17	4.23
4. More Help from Districts and Boards	4.42	4.48	4.39	4.48
5. Support from Universities	3.93	3.95	3.91	3.96
6. Reward & Recognition from Professional Groups	4.08	4.19	4.09	4.04
7. TOTAL Attitude toward Incentives	3.8	4.07	4.04	4.13

The tenure issue was an eye-opener when considered by district size and type. Superintendents in the smallest districts favor tenure more positively, averaging 3.54, while those from medium sized systems rated it lower at 3.32, and largest system respondents yet lower at 3.19. These findings indicate that all superintendents desire assistance, support, and better pay, while tenure is only of interest to those superintendents in the least bureaucratic, least unionized areas (rural and small towns).

In fact, superintendents from the smallest districts tended to favor more of these practical steps than their colleagues in the larger systems. This difference may indicate a sense of isolation, a lack of competitive pay and perks, and the need for more external assistance from their boards and neighboring universities for local superintendents. As earlier data show (see Table 3), superintendents in smaller districts appear most mobile, indicating a willingness to take another position if one were available. Perhaps because these school executives tend to be younger than larger system leaders, they appear more willing to entertain the idea of changing jobs and accepting the next challenge.

Implications and Recommendations?

These and the other findings and implications from this study point to several recommendations for improving the future of the superintendency:

1. Create job paths across districts by size and location: Our data show the mobility limitations of treating the superintendency market as unitary or uni-dimensional. We see, instead, sub-markets, based on the type and location of districts, which impose barriers to superintendents' seeking jobs in districts very much different from where they were originally socialized.

We thus recommend devices for exposing candidates to different kinds of districts to broaden and enrich the pool. One way would be to develop "career development programs" that allow superintendents (or those wishing to join the profession) to experience life in very different districts. For example, states, working with AASA and other national groups (e.g., the National School Boards Association and the Council of Great City Schools), could organize high-profile internships and visiting leaders programs to entice small district leaders to consider working in larger, more urbanized systems. Such programs could enlarge the pool and provide springboards for candidates to test themselves in districts that they might not otherwise consider.

2. Reorganize the superintendency: Another change indicated by this study is the need to make the post more attractive, secure, and manageable. Respondents would like to see, for instance, more support from the district, clearer expectations, better pay related to increases in other fields and among teachers and principals, more help and assistance from universities, and greater chances to be recognized for work well done.

One possible approach is for districts to create management teams around key goals (e.g., better curriculum and instruction, more efficient use of resources, better relations with community and parents, increased staff growth and development for teachers), and then ask the superintendent to serve as the coordinator and sounding-board for these groups. By shifting some of the skill areas to those closest to schools and students, and making it the superintendent's job to listen and react, rather than to control and supervise, school district leaders could stop trying to be everywhere and do everything, an impossible task that leads to feelings of incompetence and frustration.

3. Expand superintendents' pension opportunities: The nation as a whole, working with the U.S. Department of Education and the various national associations (e.g., teachers, principals, school boards, superintendents, Education Commission of the States), should work toward a national retirement program or at least reciprocity among states, whereby superintendents who seek and gain employment in one state can "take their pension with them" when moving to another. This change would certainly increase mobility across lines, and would increase the job pool considerably. University professors and other employees have the TIAA-CREFF system, which is national and allows enrollees to carry their pensions to other participating institutions (in any state).

If a national scheme is too radical, perhaps regional agreements among states in New England, the Middle Atlantic States, South, Midwest, Southwest, and Pacific states would provide greater regional mobility and a larger pool of superintendent candidates.

4. Expand and improve doctoral programs -- and other training opportunities -- for superintendents: The survey shows that fully 64 percent of the superintendents in this study had their doctorate, with the highest percentage of large district superintendents holding a doctorate and the lowest percentage found among small district superintendents. Three recommendations emerge from this finding.

First, future educators interested in becoming superintendents will likely need an Ed.D. or Ph.D. Degree availability is not universal, however; leaders who live in more isolated areas of the country and work in smaller systems are, according to our data, *half as likely* to have their doctorate as large district administrators. Hence, the need is obvious to make these degrees not only high quality, but also available to all school leaders. We would suggest state or national scholarships for rural superintendents to allow them the resources and time off to study for the advanced degree. Equity suggests giving these education executives the same chances as their more metropolitan, cosmopolitan colleagues.

Second, since it seems that most superintendents will be getting the doctoral degree in the future, we urge professors of educational administration to reconsider the content and skills base of the many doctoral programs in school administration. We urge thoughtful discussion of questions such as: To what extent do these programs focus on the vision, values, processes, standards, and results of leading the modern school system? What might be done to make these degree programs stronger, both in conceptualizing the job and in performing it?

Obvious changes are already underway, which include closer ties between school districts and university programs; courses that stress best practices as well as the latest concepts; and dissertations more related to both theory and practice, but more needs to be done.

Third, professors of educational administration should include (or increase) in their programs elements traditionally associated with other degrees, such as business administration and law. As the structure of U.S. education changes -- with charter schools, vouchers, inter-district school admissions, out-sourcing of key education services, home education, and even the rise of the "virtual school" (i.e., students studying via the computer at home, in their work place, or at a museum) -- the role of chief education officer will change from that of top executive to chief entrepreneur: someone seeking to "service" the range of public, quasi-public, private, and privatized schools rather than to control or manage them. Sales and service may take precedence over management and control. Leaders need new skills -- and their graduate programs must help them acquire these skills.

5. Address the economic concerns of superintendents: The data show a high concern for the economics of the position, given that teachers now earn between $40,000 and $75,000 for 10 months work, and building principals, between $58,000 and $115,000 in some areas of the country. Why would large numbers of leaders seek a superintendency when such high pay is available for other educators (teachers, principals, librarians, or guidance personnel) who work fewer months and have greater job security and fewer headaches?

This survey asked a number of questions about the financial rewards and incentives of the superintendency. The diminution of the pay differential between their roles and top-paid teachers and administrators and salary capping were of real concern to respondents, especially those in the small districts.

Clearly, in many places, the salaries have not kept pace with either inflation or the rising pay for other educators. But our data do not show those in the top jobs to be a greedy group. In fact, Table 18 shows that respondents desire district help and support just as much as better pay and benefits. Being able to do the job well, to be recognized, and to have a fulfilling career are key concerns. Better pay is important, but not enough. Still, it seems logical that to attract quality candidates to the superintendency in the future, school systems are likely to have to increase salary, benefits and perks.

Further research is necessary to get a better sense of superintendents' financial needs.

6. Be aware of the changing role of the superintendent as a family member and its effect on mobility: As the next generation assumes the role of superintendent, the "new family" will also have an effect. Our data indicate that family issues, such as moving the family to another location, finding a spouse a job, or leaving friends and family behind, were of moderate concern to respondents. But, as men and women assume greater economic and job parity, and spouses of superintendents have their own jobs and careers, it may become even more difficult to relocate to another region or state. This development may mean more districts will have to promote from within (the so-called "place-bound" superintendent; see Carlson, 1966) rather than seeking to import candidates from outside the district or region. Again, this tendency to "go local" will have a profound effect on the isolated rural and small town districts, which have smaller talent pools from which to promote.

Already we see the rise of the interim superintendent -- someone placed in the position for three months to a year to give the district and school board time to select a permanent candidate. An increasing number of school systems are either between superintendents or · have made interim appointments as they struggle to define their needs, locate acceptable candidates, and settle on a choice. The choice of an interim superintendent puts the district "on hold" and often leads to the appointment of interim principals and other staff, leaving it up to the permanent leaders, whenever they arrive, to quickly make hard personnel and program decisions.

Whatever the results, if districts hope to recruit new, talented, and younger superintendents, the problems of relocating must be addressed. Like executive searches in industry, the hunt for the best superintendent must rightly include the spouse and children -- and selling the entire family on the advantages of moving to the district.

7. Increase opportunities for women and minorities: In the first half of the 20th century, women were underrepresented in the superintendency. "In the latter half of the 20th century, the almost invisible woman superintendent is again claiming a visible space" according to Patricia A. Schmuck (1999, p. ix). While Glass (1992) and others found only about 6 percent of superintendents were women in 1992, by 1999 in our stratified random sample, the percentage of female superintendents had risen to 12.2 percent, perhaps because we skewed the sample toward larger districts.

Our data show women having apparently greater opportunity in the larger school systems, the urban centers, than in small and medium (suburban) districts. With 12.2 percent of the total survey population female, larger districts had 22.7 percent female superintendents, medium districts about 12.5 percent, and small districts only 10.1.

AASA data (Glass, 1992) show that only 4 percent of superintendents at the beginning of the 1990s were African American and even fewer were Latino or Asian. As our schools become more ethnically diverse, the need to promote dynamic leaders from these underrepresented communities is becoming critical (see Glass, 1993). Efforts should be made, therefore, to train, prepare, and promote women and minorities into the top leadership spots.

Perhaps states agencies, universities, and state-national organizations could create more "fast-track" programs to identify talented women and minorities (not to mention minority women) for the superintendency. Several such programs have been tried in the past, with some success, including those conducted by The Danforth Foundation and the Council of Great City Schools, as well as the Education Professions Development Act (EPDA) of the U.S. Department of Education.

8. Re-tool the skills of superintendents: Our survey data indicate that most superintendents see themselves as people-people, focusing on community relations, human relations, and, most important, relations with their school boards. In this study, 96 percent of respondents agree that their "relationship with the school board is critical in making important educational decisions."

Secondarily, these educators report having solid skills in specific areas such as budgeting, finance, staff development, curriculum design, and building construction. In other areas, such as technology and race relations, superintendents indicate a need for additional training and exposure.

Furthermore, we see changes coming in management, structure, and organizational design (e.g., the "learning organization" methods of people like Peter Senge) that call for new methods and approaches. If business leaders can attend institutes to expose themselves to the latest thinking, why can't school superintendents as well? To some degree, the change of generations might take care of concerns related to technology skills and other areas, but this remains to be seen. How the new generation will be prepared is perhaps the key question of the next century.

9. Telescope the time-consuming career steps to the superintendency: Our data show that sample superintendents worked in education for nearly 30 years, and spent more than 16 years of those years reaching the superintendency. As the process now goes, superintendents rise through the ranks in a rather long process of teaching, building-level administration, central-office service, and assistant superintendency, finally reaching the top job. One suggestion for increasing the candidate pool is to focus on the early identification of talented leaders from the ranks of education or outside the field and create high-powered training programs to groom them earlier and faster for top leadership positions in education.

10. Recognize superintendents' contributions at national, regional, state, and local levels: This survey and the high number of voluntary participants who sent in their questionnaires reflect superintendents' feelings of isolation and desire to participate in their own career development. Because it is lonely "at the top," many executives need to communicate among themselves about their lives, their careers, their aspirations, and their accomplishments. We need to realize and somehow publicize the work these educators do, and the resources they need to accomplish the great task they have undertaken.

Our study underscores the need to create ways (web sites, programs, meetings, etc.) for top leaders to share ideas, exchange solutions, and visit one another. Regional and national support systems could help alleviate superintendents' feelings of isolation and increase their effectiveness.

Final Thoughts

Our results indicate that sitting superintendents are strongly aware of a crisis in the profession, concerned about future recruiting of new and talented leaders, and worried about "turnover" in the job. But the results are not all negative. Our data also show a long-term commitment to the superintendency; a strong sense of pride and satisfaction with their accomplishments; a continuing belief that they, as superintendents, are making a difference in the lives of children; and clear signals that it is in society's best interest to recognize and promote these efforts.

The school superintendency, now over 150 years old, has grown in *importance* as public education has expended in scope, size, and accomplishments; in *complexity* as education has taken on more and more functions; and in *political exposure and vulnerability* as education is increasingly scrutinized by courts, governments, and attentive publics. Carter and Cunningham (1997) explain well the changing context of the job and the "demands and opportunities" for superintendents of the 21st century:

> The constellation of social, economic, demographic, political, and technological factors is changing the world. … Superintendents are asked to build direction, alignment, and the culture of visionaries; to encourage risk and experimentation; to set the pace; and to lead by example. Superintendents also demonstrate a deep commitment to protecting and promoting the valuable bridge between yesterday and tomorrow. (p. 238)

References

Auriemma, F. A.; Cooper, B. S., & Smith, S. (1991). *Graying Teachers.* Eugene, OR: ERIC Center for Education Management.

Blumberg, A. (1985). *The School Superintendent: Living in Conflict.* New York: Teachers College Press.

Bok, D. (1992). "Foundations Seek to Expand Pool of City School Chiefs." *Education Week 11,*20: 48.

Carlson, R.O. (1966). *Executive Succession.* Chicago: University of Chicago Press.

Carter, G.R., & Cunningham, W.G. (1997). *The American School Superintendent.* New York: Jossey-Bass.

Casserly, M. (1992). *National Urban Education Goals: Baseline Indicators, 1990-91.* ERIC Document Reproduction Service No. ED 351422.

Crowson, R.L. (1987). "The Local School District Superintendent: A Puzzling Role." *Educational Administration Quarterly 23,* 3: 49-69.

Fernandez, J. (1995). In Kowalski, T.J. (1995). *Keepers of the Flame: Contemporary Urban Superintendents.* Thousand Oaks, CA: Corwin Press.

Glass, T.E. (1992). *The 1992 Study of the American Superintendency.* Arlington, VA: American Association of School Administrators.

Glass, T.E. (1993). "Point and Counterpoint: What Is in the Context of What Might Be?" In Carter, D.S.G., Glass, T.E., & Hord, S.M. *Selecting, Preparing, and Developing the School District Superintendent.* Washington, DC: Falmer Press.

Houston, P.D. (June 3, 1998). "The ABC's of Administrative Shortages." Commentary, *Education Week* 44, 32.

Jackson, B.L. (1995). *Balancing Act: The Political Role of the Urban School Superintendent.* Washington, D. C.: Joint Center for Political and Economic Studies.

Kowalski, T.J. (1995). *Keepers of the Flame: Contemporary Urban Superintendents.* Thousand Oaks, CA: Corwin Press.

Montenegro, X. (1993). *Women and Racial Minorities in School Administration.* Arlington, VA: AASA.

Mulligan, D. (1996). "Thinking Career Move? Consider Jobs." *Central Conference Daily* Vol. 15:1-16.

Norton, M., Webb, L., Dlugosh, L., & Sybouts, W. (1996). *The School Superintendency: New Responsibilities, New Leadership.* Boston: Allyn & Bacon.

Ornstein, A.C. (1992). "School Superintendents and School Board Members: Who Are They?" *Contemporary Education 63*,2: 157-159.

Renchler, R. (1992). "Urban Superintendent Turnover: The Need for Stability." *Sounding Board* 1, 1: 1-3.

Sarason, S. (1985). "Foreword." In A. Blumberg, *The School Superintendent: Living in Conflict.* New York: Teachers College Press.

Schmuck, P.A. (1999). In *Sacred Dreams: Women and the Superintendency*, C.C. Brunner (ed.). Albany, NY: SUNY Press.

Thomas, W.B., & Moran, K.J. (1992). "Reconsidering the Power of the Superintendent in the Progressive Period." *American Educational Research Journal 29*,1: 22-50.

Appendix A

Superintendents' Professional Expectations and Advancement Review (SPEAR[TM])
Instrument

Instructions: We are concerned about the careers of superintendents and believe you may have some insights into the problems of mobility, job security, and job futures. Please fill out this questionnaire and the results will be kept strictly **confidential** and be aggregated to protect identities.

Career History. Please check (✓) or fill in the following items:

1. I am currently serving as: ( ) Superintendent of Schools ( ) Assistant Superintendent
    ( ) Other (Describe)
    _____

2. I have held this post for _____ years.

3. If a "good" job opened up in another district, would you consider applying for it?
    ( ) Yes, definitely ( ) Yes, maybe ( ) No, don't think so ( ) No definitely not

4. What was your **previous position**? ( ) Superintendent ( ) Assistant Superintendent
    ( ) Other Central Administration ( ) Principal ( ) Other (What?)
    _____

5. I was in this previous job for _____ years.

6. I am a member of: ( ) AASA ( ) State AASA ( ) Neither association

→ → → → → → → → → → → → → → → → →→ → → → → → →→ → → → → →
Please indicate the number of **years** in the following positions, including your current work.

7. Years in "central office" positions?   _____ Years

8. Years in "school site administration"?   _____ Years

9. Years in the "classroom"?   _____ Years

→ → → → → → → → → → → → → → → →→ → → → → → →→ → → → → → →

10. Your gender?　　( ) Male　　　( ) Female

11. Your age cohort?　( ) 20-29 Years　　( ) 30-39 Years　( ) 40-49 Years
　　　　　　　　　　( ) 50-59 Years　　( ) 60 plus

12. Highest earned degree?

　　( ) Doctorate　( ) Masters-Plus　( ) MA/MS　( ) BA/BS　( ) Other (What)?
　　_____

→ → → → → → → → → → → → → → → → →→ → → → → → →→ → → → → →

In questions 13-17, please indicate the types of superintendencies to which you are attracted. Circle your level of attraction as follows:

3 = high attraction　　2 = moderate attraction　1 = low attraction　　0 = no attraction

13.	Rural district	3	2	1	0
14.	Large, urban district	3	2	1	0
15.	Suburban district	3	2	1	0
16.	Inner city district	3	2	1	0
17.	District similar to my present position	3	2	1	0

→ → → → → → → → → → → → → → → →→ → → → → → →→ → → → → →

Superintendent Specialization

In questions 18-27, please indicate the levels of your professional expertise as superintendent. Circle the level as follows:

3 = high expertise　2 = moderate expertise　　1 = low expertise　　0 = no expertise

18.	Construction/bond issues	3	2	1	0
19.	Human relations	3	2	1	0
20.	Labor relations	3	2	1	0
21.	Race relations	3	2	1	0
22.	Curriculum design	3	2	1	0
23.	Staff development	3	2	1	0
24.	Finance/budget	3	2	1	0
25.	Working with the community	3	2	1	0

26.   Integration of technology   3   2   1   0

27.   Other (What?) _____   3   2   1   0

→ →

28.   Are you vested in the **pension** at your current job?   ( ) Yes   ( ) No

29.   If not, in how many years will you be vested?   _____ Years

30.   In how many states do you have a pension?   _____ States

31.   If you have relocated to another state, would you consider returning to the state where you have accumulated the most pension?   ( ) Yes   ( ) No

32.   Approximately how many **students** do you have in your district? _____ Student enrollment

33.   How many **schools**?

        _____ Elementary _____ Middle/Jr. High _____ High School _____ Other _____ Total

34.   What is your school district's **location**? (Check one)

        ( ) Urban   ( ) Suburban   ( ) Small town   ( ) Other

35.   Your district is in what **state**?   State of _____

36   Approximately what percent of your district's **students** are?

        ( ) % American Indian/Alaskan Native ( ) % Black   ( ) % Hispanic
        ( )% Asian or Pacific Islander   ( ) % White

37. Approximately what percent of students in your district qualify for free and assisted lunch? ___%

→ →

Please respond to the following statements concerning job applicants by indicating one of these responses for each item:

5 = AGREE strongly   4 = AGREE somewhat 3 = Neither AGREE or DISAGREE
2 = DISAGREE somewhat   1 = DISAGREE strongly

Crisis in the School Superintendency?

(Please circle one number per statement)

38.	The shortage of applicants for superintendents' jobs is a serious crisis in American education.	5	4	3	2	1
39.	A crisis in school leadership is created by the low quality of candidates for the superintendency.	5	4	3	2	1
40.	High turnover for the superintendency means a serious crisis in keeping strong leaders in the position	5	4	3	2	1

Economic Roots of the Crisis?

41.	The lack of pension portability is a strong economic disincentive in my not applying for a superintendency in another part of the state or country	5	4	3	2	1
42.	Low level of pay is at the economic root of why candidates may not seek a superintendency in another district.	5	4	3	2	1
43.	Economic supports (perks such as housing and car allowances and annuities) are just not there for the superintendency.	5	4	3	2	1
44.	The cost of living (i.e., buying a house in another district) is a strong economic factor in my not applying for a superintendency in another region of the state or country.	5	4	3	2	1
45.	The pay differential for superintendents (when compared to senior-level teachers and building administrators) has seriously diminished the economic attractiveness of the superintendency.	5	4	3	2	1
46.	The tendency of communities to cap the raises for superintendents is a real economic concern when considering a job change.	5	4	3	2	1

Career Satisfaction

47.	When applying for a new superintendency, the challenge of taking on the leadership of a tough school district and making improvements would increase my career satisfaction.	5	4	3	2	1
48.	My work in this district has given me real career satisfaction.	5	4	3	2	1
49.	The loss of prestige of the superintendency over the years has diminished my job satisfaction.	5	4	3	2	1

50.	In advising fellow educators, I would truly recommend the profession of superintendent of schools as a meaningful and satisfying career.	5	4	3	2	1
51.	Successful changes in curriculum, teaching and testing give me a real sense of career satisfaction.	5	4	3	2	1

Personal Incentives

52.	I was personally motivated in my decision to become a superintendent by the authority and status associated with the job.	5	4	3	2	1
53.	The opportunity to make a significant difference in the lives of children was a strong personal incentive for my becoming a superintendent.	5	4	3	2	1
54.	The high risks are balanced by high rewards, and this is a consideration when weighing whether to apply for a new superintendency.	5	4	3	2	1

Family-Related Concerns

55.	Moving my family is not a problem for me when applying for new jobs in other regions.	5	4	3	2	1
56.	When considering a new superintendency outside the region, the problem of locating a job for my spouse is a serious familial concern.	5	4	3	2	1
57.	Proximity to relatives and friends is a consideration when applying for a new superintendency.	5	4	3	2	1

Job Organization and Decision-Making

		5	4	3	2	1
58.	The job organization of superintendent is too demanding of time and energy to attract new and talented candidates to the position.	5	4	3	2	1
59.	My relationship with the school board is critical to me in making important educational decisions.	5	4	3	2	1
60.	Turnover on the school board affects my decision-making process.	5	4	3	2	1
61.	The organizational and legal constraints of government regulation and teacher contracts prevent me as superintendent from fulfilling my job potential.	5	4	3	2	1

Superintendent Recruitment Incentives

		5	4	3	2	1
62.	Tenure for the superintendency would bring more candidates into the applicant pool.	5	4	3	2	1
63.	Higher pay and better benefits would be a strong incentive to candidates in considering a career in the superintendency.	5	4	3	2	1
64.	Better perks (housing, car, more trips to professional meetings) could help to bring more candidates into the applicant pool.	5	4	3	2	1
65.	Districts should consider giving current superintendents more help and support to ensure their well-being and job success.	5	4	3	2	1
66.	Universities and other institutions should assist candidates in preparing for job growth and promotion through, for example, training and counseling.	5	4	3	2	1
67.	Professional and state education organizations should do more to support, recognize and reward the accomplishments of superintendents.	5	4	3	2	1

→ →

⇨ Thank you for participating. We shall send a summary of our findings to all participants.

⇨ Supported by the American Association of School Administrators (AASA).

DO NOT USE OR REPRODUCE WITHOUT PERMISSION OF THE AUTHORS AND AASA.

→ →

Fordham University Superintendents' Career Study
Vincent Carella & Bruce S. Cooper
Fordham University
School of Education
113 W. 60ᵗʰ Street, Room 1119
New York, NY 10023